A SPECIAL GIFT

A SPECIAL GIFT:

The Story of Jan

T. de VRIES-KRUYT

Peter H. Wyden/Publisher

NEW YORK

A Special Gift: The Story of Jan

Copyright © 1966 by Contact-Amsterdam

English translation © 1971 by T. de Vries-Kruyt

Published in Great Britain
under the title

Small Ship, Great Sea

Library of Congress Catalog Card Number: 74-76906
ISBN: 0-88326-072-7
Manufactured in the United States of America

Foreword

In 1940 Jan de Vries was born to young parents, eager and hopeful. From the time of birth, something appeared to be wrong with the little boy but a definite diagnosis of Down's Syndrome was not made until the infant was 8 months old. The parents were told it would be best to institutionalize the child, but they disregarded this advice and kept him home. With their love and concern, their foresight for the child, yet with very little professional help, they raised a boy who spoke well, could read and write, understood music, took photographs, understood religious instruction and was confirmed, and contributed fully to their family life. And this was achieved despite World War II privations and uncertainties, and in spite of their child's many additional medical problems (diabetes, numerous infections and accidents), which often received much more primitive treatment than we would give them today.

At the time of Jan's birth, most members of the medical profession generally believed that very little could be done for Down's Syndrome children, and that the development of a child such as Jan Maarten was unexpected and rather unusual. As late as 1954, a paper entitled "Two mongols of unusually high mental status" described patients with Stanford-Binet Intelligence Quotient scores of 42 and 44.

In 1959 a new interest and new look at the potential for Down's Syndrome children developed after a group of French medical researchers (headed by Dr. Lejeune) described the presence of an extra chromosome in the white cells of the blood of these patients. Chromosomes in humans are usually in pairs. The extra chromosome in these patients was thought to be a third copy of the two chromosomes of the twenty-first pair: hence the name "trisomy 21," meaning 3 twenty-first chromosomes. We now know that most of these patients can function in the moderately retarded range and that a very significant proportion of them are only mildly retarded. A patient with an I.Q. of 74 was described by Dr. Zellweger and his colleagues in 1968.

Over 90% of the patients who are called mongols and are medically classified as having Down's Syndrome have this extra chromosome. There are three other very rare forms of Down's Syndrome: 1) "mosaic" patients, with a mixture of normal and trisomic 21 cells in their blood; 2) "translocation" patients, all of whose blood cells contain a very large "double" chromosome, probably an extra 21 chromosome attached to another normal chromosome; and 3) "double chromosomal" patients who have several chromosome errors at the same time.

There is no way to be sure of a chromosomal type except by actually studying the chromosomes in the blood of the individual child. Although no patient with the trisomy-21 form of Down's Syndrome has yet been recorded in the normal I.Q. range, a small percentage of the patients with the mosaic and translocation forms of Down's Syndrome have been found to have normal levels of intelligence. Jan appears to have been functioning in the mildly retarded range—so he could have had any of the different types of Down's Syndrome.

We may not know Jan Maarten's exact chromosomal type but we do know that he had an opportunity to develop his potential as an individual human being because of the way he was raised with his family. It is now apparent that environmental factors can critically alter the expression of a child's developmental potential. In 1964 a study by Shotwell and Shipe demonstrated that Down's Syndrome infants reared at home during the first two years of life had superior intellectual and social development compared with those children placed in an institution soon after birth. There has been an increasing number of other studies confirming and emphasizing these results. Today, most pediatricians do not recommend institutional placement of a newborn Down's Syndrome baby; many public institutions for the retarded are reluctant to accept a newborn baby. Infant stimulation programs and special environmental enriching and training programs for older Down's Syndrome children have shown that there is a great range and variety of potential among these youngsters. Another vital consideration is the fact that lifetime institutionalization for a child today in the United States may run to between $100,000 and $200,000 per patient. What is most important is that each child needs to be considered as an individual and worked with as an individual. Even institutionalized patients can have their potential modified by special training. At Sonoma State Hospital in California, for example, a number of mongoloid children underwent an intensive program of language stimulation and were taught to read; this resulted in their eventual discharge from the institution and return to the community, where they were able to attend special education classes in the public schools.

In retarded patients, such as those with Down's Syndrome, one sees in exaggerated form the principles that actually apply to all children. Any child blossoms, growing in intelligence and maturity, with love and stimulation and with his acceptance as an individual, however nature has happened to fashion him. Any child fails to develop properly in a loveless atmosphere where parents or family reject him or he does not receive the normal amount of stimulation because of an institutional setting.

The parents of little Jan understood this, maybe intuitively, but certainly very positively. They responded to him as an individual; "his upbringing was based largely on what we discovered in the child himself," his mother writes. The following pages demonstrate that they have never regretted their decision to raise their own child and that they did an outstanding job of it. This book is both a historically interesting document and a loving testimony to the power of human caring.

Mary Coleman, M.D.

DECEMBER 1973
WASHINGTON , D.C.

Contents

I

'How Is Your Son
So Normal?'

THE restaurant at Oostergo looked particularly cheerful that day. The sun shone its best outside, and its rays were reflected into the room by the water, so that the light shimmering on the walls and over the tables created the impression of being on board ship. It was an ideal spot for a celebration, and that was what the people at the center table were doing.

The six girls were enjoying dinner with the middle-aged couple who had come over for the evening with their son to the sailing resort, where the girls were spending a holiday.

The table was noisy with stories about the school graduating examinations they had just sat, and there was also a more recent incident involving a broken mast. That they were all relaxed and happy was evident to the rest of the room, and it wasn't surprising that some of the other guests eavesdropped every now and then. The father was teasing the girls, who had obviously steered more successfully through school exams than over the local lake. As usual, the members of the crew could not agree on the cause of the accident.

3

'What do you think, Jan Maarten?' they asked the boy.

'No comment. I'm only a grade B student.'

There was a moment's silence before they all shouted with laughter at this unexpected reply. Jan sat looking very pleased with himself. His father and mother were at either end of the table. Shortly afterward the waiter asked the father if he would mind having a word with another couple sitting near the window. Of course not. As he approached the two strangers he wondered if he should know them. Was she an ex-pupil of his? (He had taught in Amsterdam during the war.) Or was the husband a business contact he did not at once recognize?

'You don't know us and we don't know you, but we have a boy just like your son. How is it that he is so "normal"?'

Jan Maarten de Vries is a backward child of the type known as 'mongoloid.' He is now in his twenties. Because of his health, he is an exceptionally fragile craft to keep afloat; yet he is a brave boy who often makes severer demands on himself than a healthy, normal person would. He is polite, happy, has a sense of humor and a well-developed sense of duty; always busy, he is a very lovable member of the family.

'How is it that your son is so "normal"?'

It is not the first time we, his parents, have been asked that question. Acquaintances who come to us

4

for advice about their backward children ask it too. The pediatrician who treated him for diabetes put it almost impatiently, imperatively.

'Your son is an average case of mongolism,' he added. 'I've known others who were much more intelligent but who have remained far more retarded. How did you stimulate his development to this extent?'

There are many children like Jan Maarten, as a visit to any school for the retarded will demonstrate. Many children are born suffering from mongolism ... And when I try to answer that question, usually asked with such a world of emotion behind it, I always think of the very young ones who still have a future before them, who still have it in them to become either a blessing or an intolerable burden.

If we answered in general terms, we would have to admit that we were lucky. We had learned to accept our griefs before Jan was a year old and were busy finding out how best we could bring him up. That was in 1941. Neither of our families had ever been confronted with an abnormal child before. The war reduced our sorrow to the proper proportions, and in those times it was a privilege to grieve over something that had not been brought about by others. There are a number of doctors in our family and many of our friends are doctors too. Not one of them has ever been reluctant to give us advice. This has saved the boy's life time and again, for such children are delicate and often react to normal illnesses so unexpectedly that only quick action can save them.

Another point in our favor was that Jan was our eldest child. It was therefore not necessary for us to alter an established pattern, geared to the needs of normal children. We had time to think about how we would solve various problems, and we took the trouble to note our mistakes and to set them right.

Yes, Jan Maarten, we were very lucky.

It is to help others find the happiness that is rooted in a great sorrow that I shall try to answer the question 'How is it that Jan is what he is?' In order to do so, I shall explore the submerged storehouse of my memories, which is something we all love to do at different times and in different moods. I once had the privilege, when skin-diving in Biak, of seeing the silent golden world past the coral reef, a fascinating world full of colors, light and dark. It is difficult to say exactly what I saw, since that depended largely on the angle at which the rays of the sun struck the water.

When I examine that brightly colored fish, Jan Maarten, in the deep-sea world of my memory, I try to find the right light that will illumine some moments in his life that may be of interest to others. Who are those others? They are all those parents with whom we feel a close bond, who want to do their best for the child who is different from others.

6

First he is everybody's plaything, everybody's darling, until almost imperceptibly he becomes a problem, a tyrant in the home. There are good institutions for these children, but they have long waiting lists. The problem grows out of all proportion. Is this necessary, must this happen with all mongoloids, or can we prevent such situations from ever developing?

It is not possible to give a universally applicable answer to this question. A great deal can be avoided if consistent attention is paid to all aspects of their upbringing. In our busy and eventful life Jan's path has not been very different from that of the rest of the family. I kept no diary of his days, but I know he never ruled our lives. Yet he always received the loving care and interest that was his due, just as the other children did. His upbringing was based largely on what we discovered in the child himself.

2

A First Son

JAN Maarten was born on October 22, 1940. He arrived well on time, weighed 5½ lbs., and resembled a lizard rather than a baby. His long, narrow tongue, too long and too narrow, moved rapidly in and out of his mouth. His eyes slanted slightly upward and there were two clearly visible folds of skin at the eyes near the bridge of his tiny nose. Mother was enchanted with the baby, but when his father first saw him, he was shocked into silence.

'Oh,' said the young gynecologist, 'you can't really tell in the beginning. Newborn babies are always so crumpled. They fill out soon enough.'

'If you're absolutely sure, I'll open a bottle of champagne. After all, it is my first son.'

The gynecologist hesitated for a fraction of a second.

'Let's not open the bottle just yet, alright?' suggested Jan's father.

The two young men, both in their early thirties, looked at each other in silence. The baby whimpered softly in the bedroom behind them.

'It's probably wiser to postpone the celebrations for a while.'

And thus the doctor admitted that he too had his doubts. It would not have been fair to have pretended at a time like this.

The father had found an ally, and together they watched the changes and developments in the child as the months went by. The mother loved the baby completely and utterly.

'You're not beautiful, but you're all mine.'

The first baby is an experience that is not easily described. This tiny, living thing in your arms depends on you wholly. Cherish it, whisper endearments while you hug its warmth to the warmth of your body—it is yours as nothing ever has been, ever before. Time stands still. Is there a future full of problems? Of course not. There is a cot with a child close by, eyes that watch you as the tiny mouth drinks. You, baby, you are the whole world to your mother and father.

The mother was able to hide behind the unescapable fact of her joy in the child as a child and in her daily care of him. Her mind registered the deviations but immediately postponed judgment. A doctor does not like to commit himself before the child's first birthday, she thought. A year, a whole year! The front door of the little house opened on the outside world and the outside world was at war.

When father and mother said goodbye to each other every morning, they did not hurry their farewells, for every parting could have been for a long, long time. How much could happen in a year! And in all that time the child was with them, was theirs.

Then the father's fears broke like a wave on the rock of the mother's happiness. He could not go on as if everything was normal, he could not be glad about something that was sure to bring unhappiness. And he was sure that the future could not be happy. A man and a woman, traveling the same *via dolorosa*, will react differently to their sorrows. But they should share them; it is not good to travel alone.

When Jan was eight months old, his father quite unexpectedly met a children's specialist, Professor Cornelia de Lange. He managed to have a talk with her and tell her of his fears. She was deeply concerned for the young teacher who confided in her, and she visited his home a week later. After examining Jan thoroughly, she stated that this was a severe case of mongolism and that the child was unlikely ever to be able to walk or talk. She advised his father not to keep him at home but to look around for a good institution in which to place him as soon as possible. She also strongly advised him against telling the mother. 'Let her come to realize it herself.'

The father took Professor de Lange home and then tried to live with this knowledge that he alone had. Fortunately, he did not succeed too well, and there came a time when both parents were forced to face a catastrophe which they had no choice but to accept and to learn to live with.

Outside their small home the war went on, bringing to each individual his own personal tragedies, sometimes small, sometimes overwhelming.

'Hasn't God given us our grief in a very dear form?' It was this thought which crystallized in the minds of the father and mother after a while. And because they were both very active people, they started discussing what they could actually do, what was humanly possible to stimulate Jan's development.

The summer of 1941 found them in a cottage on the shores of a lake. For a Friesian yacht was the third party in the happy triangle of their marriage. It was all the young couple possessed, and every holiday was built round this single worldly treasure. The wide, flat meadows of Holland stretched out around the playpen in which Jan began to develop his first activities. Had the air of a big city disagreed with him? Was the seafaring blood inherited from his father beginning to stir in his veins? The quiet, apathetic baby was becoming lively and started crawling with gusto.

In September his father and mother decided to

consult a pediatrician, since it was obvious that they would need expert advice regularly. They chose a specialist who had studied medicine with Jan's grandfather, and he was relieved at being able to speak his mind quite openly to the young couple. They kept themselves carefully in check; they wanted to know the worst, but they also wanted to know how much they dared to hope. In the two months that had passed since Professor de Lange's visit, Jan had grown into a lively, cheerful baby. So the prospects the doctor now unfolded were not as somber as they had once been.

'These children are fond of music, they can learn to talk a little, they are very lovable but they are also very delicate. You really shouldn't count on the little boy's reaching his ninth year.' And then came the point which he went into most deeply. 'Do not keep the child at home. There are excellent institutions where such children are really happy. It isn't easy to send the child away, but it is better to do so. Better for the mother and better for the other children, when there are other children in the family.'

We all know that bad burns are seldom immediately painful. And this new knowledge was like a bad burn. So the father and mother were able to carry on the conversation with deceptive ease, but it took time to accept these facts, and the process of acceptance was a painful one. However, the young couple again proved that the truth sets you free. It is *good* to know the worst. Every thinking person has a right to know it. It is not easy to arrive at conclusions about things it hurts even to talk about. Yet it is not always kindness to spare another's feelings—you could start sparing your own. On the other hand, some decisions need time to mature. And when they are put into words they often seem surprisingly simple.

The mother and father came to two conclusions in a comparatively short time. They formulated them as promises, which they have always kept, and worded them something like this:

'If it is not granted us to keep this child for long, let us consciously each day enjoy every lovely thing he brings us and let us not plan too far ahead.'

This then was an interpretation of 'have no care for the morrow,' which Jan taught them to respect. It helped them to experience each moment intensely and with the utmost perception. It was a decision on which to some extent they based the philosophy of life which supported them in good times and in bad. The second promise concerned the straightforward advice not to keep Jan at home.

'If ever our home should come to resemble a hospital or if the other children should in any way suffer from their brother's handicap, then Jan Maarten will have to go to an institution. We shall look around for a suitable one, so that if and when the time comes for him to go we shall not have to make decisions in a hurry. But as long as the problems are only organizational ones, we shall not avoid them, but will tackle them boldly.'

The two young people felt strangely at peace, actively at peace, if that were possible, and very close to each other. They were safe in the knowledge that underneath them were the Everlasting Arms, and that gave them strength, even in time of war.

3

Learning and Growing

THE pediatrician glanced quickly round the room.

'That little table in the corner is rather low for a child like this,' was his practical advice. 'And I doubt whether books so near the ground will be safe ... However, you must see how it works out. Prevention is better than cure.'

Opinons differ as to when the wisdom of a proverb should be put into practice. Jan had soon learned to crawl in the lakeside cottage. Back in the apartment in town a gate was fitted at the top of the stairs, but no other alterations were made. A few days after their return home, Jan's mother found him beside the bookcase, picking at the cover of one of the books. She sat down beside him, took his chubby little hand and smacked it gently.

'Don't do that,' she said firmly, and put the book back on the shelf.

Jan Maarten was deposited elsewhere in the room with a toy. His mother went to the kitchen, and when she returned he was again poking in the bookcase but looked up as she came in.

'Don't do that,' she repeated calmly, picked him

up and put him in his playpen. This gave him food for thought, but after a while he turned round and started playing with the toys in the playpen.

Thus the pattern evolved naturally. A light smack on the hand unmistakably linked with the 'sin' committed was the first step, prompt removal to the playpen the second. His mother found that it was very little trouble to teach him what was allowed and what was not. The golden rule was always to act in the same way even when he only 'tried it on.' He would sometimes sit near the bookcase and look at her. Then he looked at his hand, again at his mother and then slowly reached out for his favorite book. As soon as he touched it, retribution would follow in the form of a rap over the knuckles and a stern 'Don't do that!' (accompanied, of course, by a perfectly straight face). He always seemed relieved that the sequence of events occurred as he had expected.

When the first snowflakes of the severe winter of 1942 started falling in February, the coal shortage in the Province of Utrecht drove three small cousins to the refuge of the warm apartment where Jan and his parents lived. There were twins, just turned two, and a 'big' boy of four.

For the first time Jan's universal goodwill expressed itself in a violent preference for certain individuals. He could not share the playpen with the

one twin who would not leave him alone, whereas
his relations with the other twin were quite normal.
During the two months that the cold kept those
welcome but involuntary guests, Jan's forehead was
covered with bruises. After all, affection expressed
with wooden blocks is apt to leave its mark. Apart
from this, all went well.

The mother saw in these weeks that Jan learned
best by imitating. The twins were not yet toilet-
trained, so Jan learned the proper use of the pot
together with them, encouraged by sincere and fer-
vent praise for their united efforts. The snow, the
sledge, the many coats and caps did not cause any
problems because there were always four little boys
who were always doing the same thing. It was a
happy time, and Jan missed his cousins sadly when
they left.

What had he learned from them? It was difficult
to put it into words. He had shared completely in
their games and quarrels; they had knocked him
down and put him on his feet again. They had
snatched away his toys and given them back
again—sometimes. He had learned a number of
things *with* them, so his mother realized that it was
easier for him that way. But above all Jan had
learned that in a community, however small, every
member must be tolerant. Where can you learn that
better than in the restricted space of a playpen?

In May 1942 the family returned to the lakeside

cottage. Jan's health again improved greatly, as it had the year before. Then he had learned to crawl, now he learned to walk. There were always guests coming and going at the cottage, which was not surprising, since it was a lovely spot and accessible by bicycle from town. Everyone was welcome and there was always room for one extra at table and almost always a bed in the attic. Jan was an easy child. He was willing to be fed by one or other of the guests if his mother was busy and he was uniformly cheerful with almost everyone. Yet just as he sometimes showed a marked preference for one person, so he also could react violently against another. He once gave a visitor a well-aimed smack with his little arm, while his whole body expressed resistance. *These isolated incidents were memorable because they were easily explainable: in every case the person concerned was someone who was upset at the sight of an abnormal child.*

It is wise to remember that almost everybody experiences a shock on being confronted unexpectedly with a mongoloid child. Almost every normal person must make some mental adjustment to a greater or lesser degree, and some find it difficult. Jan's reactions were inevitably hostile to the non-adjustors, and this was painful, considering his unusual friendliness. It was a strange conflict, fought out solely at the emotional level.

His mother remembers with gratitude a touching episode dating from this period. An elderly and valued friend of the family kneels somewhat stiffly at the playpen. The living room is empty and Jan looks at her somewhat suspiciously.

'I think it is high time that you and I became friends,' she says. 'Shall I fetch that little duck for you?' It is probably the first time in her life that she has spoken to a small child. Jan relaxes, and when his mother comes into the room he is busy throwing blocks out of the playpen for his new friend to pick up. Afterward she says, rather shyly, 'I've brought a Beatrix Potter picture for him. Could you hang it up where he can see it in his room? It might appeal to him.'

Since then they have become firm friends and have always got on well together, but who can tell what our friend had to overcome in herself before she could win the trust of a mongoloid child?

The parents of the Jan Maartens of this world are very sensitive, but we must not forget that it is not always easy for others when suddenly confronted by what to us is both familiar and dear.

There were two children aged nine and five in the neighborhood who loved coming to play with little Jan. They sat outside on a big brown tarpaulin on the lawn and for hours on end encouraged him to walk.

'Come along, Jan Maarten, come to me. Oh,

careful, don't fall. Come along now. No, Jan, you mustn't crawl. Naughty boy.'

They never tired of teaching him. Sometimes they went rowing together or sailing, but Jan remained the big attraction, even though he did not seem to make much progress on the uneven grass. However, one day during a thunderstorm came the big surprise. Everyone had rushed inside while lightning flashed over the lake against a sky as black as ink and the rain still held off. The children sat on the floor with Jan. They had had to break off their favorite game but now that all the grown-ups were safely settled with cups of tea, they went on as if nothing had happened.

'Jan, come along, Jan Maarten. Ooh, aren't you a big boy now!'

The grown-ups looked up, surprised at the warm, proud, motherly tones of the nine-year old girl. 'There you are, love. You walk to Eppie now.' Carefully but confidently Jan moved his feet in the direction of her little brother. He always found in success and applause enormous stimulus and, after all, he was by no means unique in that. He practiced with admirable perseverance, and before long he was able to walk well outside too and go shopping with his mother.

Now that he was walking, a new problem arose at the lakeside cottage: *water*. Up to now water had been a great friend. Jan loved to go sailing with his parents. He was then put into the harness belonging to his high chair, which was fastened to the sheet-block with a fairly long rope. In this way he could climb onto the seat on either side of the boat. Of course he occasionally slid off, but he was astonishingly brave and he learned from his bruises. From his earliest years he seemed to have a sixth sense which warned him in precarious situations and which prompted him to act always in the same way whatever happened. He kept himself in the background, let the grown-ups cope with the situation, did exactly what he was told and did not utter a sound.

'Sit still and don't whine.'

Was it the intonation of the voice? Whatever it was, he understood. When the sail had to be taken in suddenly because of a faulty maneuver, when mother rushed from one end of the boat to the other and father had his hands full, Jan sat as quiet as a mouse, almost invisible under the mainsail. And when the sail was hoisted again, the yachtsmen remembered the existence of their exemplary son, who was calmly trying to stand up, now that the barometer seemed to indicate fair again.

'You're a jolly good sailor,' said his father proudly. Yes, water was a friend. But at the cottage there was no fence between the garden and the water, so a more spacious version of his playpen was fixed up on the lawn with a brown tarpaulin on the ground to keep out the damp. Jan hated it and obviously found it just as restrictive as the playpen itself, even though it was ten times bigger. 'He'll just have to yell,' said his mother, unmoved. 'He must get used to it. When I'm busy in the house in the morning he'll have to stay put in there.'

His father tried another method. When Jan came too near the water he warned him once in the words the child now knew all too well.

'Don't do that, Jan Maarten.'

Jan Maarten hesitated, took a few small, hesitant, yet provocative steps forward and tumbled into the water. His father rescued him in a moment and handed him over, saturated and screaming with fright, to his mother. The boy learned simple lessons like this very easily. From then on he kept a safe distance from the water's edge. Two years afterward he was to pull his younger sister, yelling with rage, away from this danger zone.

Since Jan's father had promised Professor de Lange that he would bring the child in for another examination in a year's time, the three of them made a trip to town, which Jan regarded as a great adventure. He trotted into the doctor's consulting rooms between his father and mother, such a bright little figure, but the friendly, gray-haired woman did not commit herself before she had examined him thoroughly. She was very satisfied with the progress he had made and was more hopeful for the future than she had been a year ago, although he had really been too young then for a definite opinion to be formed. His father and mother have been grateful ever since for the frank yet encouraging talk they were privileged to have with this exceptional woman.

At the end of August an entirely new element entered Jan's young life. His mother was asked if she could come immediately to fetch a Jewish baby who was being passed from hand to hand and was to have been taken care of by a friend of Jan's parents. But that friend now lay seriously ill in hospital and the child had to be helped.

Jan's mother cycled to the address she had been given and brought the baby home in a shopping bag. Jan now had a sister of his own age. In town the little Jewish girl had always been in danger of being taken away by the German occupiers and so had been kept in a cot as much as possible. Although quite normal and in fact highly intelligent, she could scarcely sit up alone. Nor had she yet learned to crawl. She obviously felt deeply insecure and cried despairingly for hours on end. Jan's mother began by trying to make her feel safe, taking her in her arms, singing to her, making little jokes. The tears dried up after a while, but the child would not let the mother out of her sight. Life had already taught her to mistrust the briefest absence. So mother lifted the child onto her hip and carried her around the house wherever she went. She was determined that the little girl should learn to stop crying, that the feeling that she was safe should grow into certainty.

Jan found the situation rather bewildering at first. He seemed to like the little girl, but of course it was difficult to prevent his feeling neglected. His mother did indeed have two hips, but could hardly get on with her housework carrying two children around with her. Fortunately, it soon became evident that Jan was going to be an important aid on the road to normality for this child who had been deprived in every possible way. Young as she was, she quickly realized that what he could do, she could do too. It annoyed her to see him stand up whenever he heard the cookie jar rattle and move in the direction of that tempting sound. She learned to crawl in record time and was soon standing up on her tiny legs. Jealousy proved a powerful stimulus.

After six weeks the real foster mother arrived, rather pale but quite ready to take charge of the little girl. It was better not to transfer the child immediately to yet other surroundings, so Jan and his parents spent another fortnight in the cottage. When they went back to town, the new foster mother and child were to stay on in the cottage. Those few weeks were unforgettable.

Jan was a good-natured child who liked a joke. For the first time in his life he had someone to play with on his own level. The two children understood each other and had fun together about things that were a mystery to the grown-ups. One evening they sat together on his mother's bed playing peek-a-boo with a minute pair of pants belonging to the little girl. Their laughter was heart-warming.

Jan Maarten turned two during this period, and his father was to bring a real birthday cake from town. When mother opened the box a sticky ruin met her eye. Father was indignant. After all, he had held the box upside down only once and then only for a short time—it had no business to collapse like that! After some ingenious plastering the damage was repaired and an impressive cake appeared on the table. Jan raised both hands above his head in speechless joy. His cake? Really for him? He brought his hands down hard, right in the middle of the cake, from sheer happiness. There must have been a jinx on it!

The departure for town could no longer be postponed, for Jan's real sister began to show signs of her arrival. What with one thing and another, it was an

eventful autumn for Jan. The nurse was rather
awkward with the little mongoloid child, and
mother was of course confined to her bed for the first
few days and did not have much time for him. He
reacted by wetting his bed. He also became restless
at night, as he had been after the little Jewish girl's
arrival. Then too there had been an unquiet two
weeks, during which he had kicked his blankets aside
and knocked his head rhythmically against the side
of his crib. His parents were not used to such
behavior; until now he had spoiled them, for even
when the house had been so full of guests that his cot
had had to be moved into the passage at night, he
had not lost a moment's sleep.

As soon as the mother was up and about again, he
stopped wetting. She was greatly relieved to discover
that this lapse was his way of taking revenge for the
neglect he must have felt directly after his sister's
birth. She silently thanked her temporary foster
child for helping her to realize Jan's great need for
her constant, loving attention. He never showed any
signs of aggressive jealousy toward his little sister.
On the contrary, he considered himself her protec-
tor, especially when he was allowed to hold her in his
chubby little arms.

That winter Jan started playing with blocks for
hours on end. He would unwearyingly build the
most improbable towers. His father and mother,
both of whom had studied physics, were astonished

at his achievements and positively relieved when the structures eventually collapsed. But he would immediately start all over again, and with great perseverance he taught himself to build his edifices higher and higher. He also derived evident pleasure from music at this stage. His parents acquired a piano, which was a tremendous success. He marched in time and with a true sense of rhythm to the many tunes that were played, chanting gruffly in his deep little voice. It was the beginning of a firm friendship with music, which for him meant mainly rhythm and movement.

His days were busy that winter, since he could now go shopping with his mother in the neighborhood. The baker, the butcher, the grocer all lived just around the corner, close enough to home for him to exercise his little legs getting there and back. This meant his first introduction to the world outside the shelter of home. The year before, when he was still in his stroller, he had attracted much less notice. There were a lot of children in the neighborhood, and his mother considered it important that they should understand Jan. Whenever she passed a group of children playing in the street and they suddenly stopped to stare at the little boy, she would make a point of not hurrying by. She always stopped and let him go up to them, as he invariably wanted to do. She would tell the children his name and ask them theirs.

'Is he ill?' they would ask. 'What's the matter with him?'

The children were naturally interested and asked their questions in a spontaneous, friendly way.

'No, he isn't ill,' his mother would then answer. 'But he isn't like you and me. He'll never be a big boy like Leo there. He was born like this. It's a pity, but he is a dear little boy. He has a heart of gold.'

The children would look at him again with interest. His mother remembers that not a single child ever showed a sign of revulsion when confronted with the abnormal boy, as some adults did. Nor did they ever tease him. The children explained to one another what was the matter with him, were always friendly toward him and soon came to accept him completely. Sometimes they worried about him, thinking that his mother did not look after him carefully enough.

Mother came to realize that she would never have got to know so many children if it had not been for Jan, nor would she have seen the best side of their nature, as she did. Once a little girl of five was waiting for her at the lamp-post at the corner, pretending to play hopscotch.

'Can't he ever get better?' she asked earnestly, like one grown-up to another.

'No,' said his mother, 'no, that's not possible.'

'But I think that's awful,' she cried out indignantly, with tears in her eyes.

'So do I,' said his mother. 'But you must remember one thing. You and I can be unhappy about it, but look at him. He's very happy, he really is never sad. He laughs and enjoys life. Then we mustn't be sad either, must we?'

The little girl hopped a few steps, pondering deeply. She sighed and said: 'No, not really, eh Jan?' and she bent over him with a gentle, motherly, protective gesture that was moving to see. There is much to learn from a five-year-old.

Father and mother both came from big families, so Jan had many cousins, some older, some younger, all of whom liked coming to stay. They played with, and especially around, Jan. When they were of the age of the little girl at the lamp-post, mother would explain to them about the boy. They inevitably appreciated this and often wanted to ask questions about certain things that bothered them. These talks invariably contributed to the success of their visit. It was as if the 'Jan Maarten question' could now be put among the problems settled satisfactorily in their minds.

He met not only the children in the neighborhood, but the adults too. Sometimes, when a group of women stood discussing the latest news on the street corner, Jan would suddenly squeeze his way into the middle of the circle with an expression on his face which clearly said, 'If there's anything interesting going on here, I'd like to know what it is!' His mother found these situations painful, but the child was so quick and often wriggled out of her grasp before she realized what he was doing. But the sequel to his behavior was invariably the same: the strained, worried faces relaxed as they looked down at the little mongoloid child. Even their voices sounded friendlier.

'Hello, sonny,' 'Oh, poor lamb!' 'Well, what have you got to say, my lad?'

His mother nodded gratefully to them as she picked up the stray 'lamb.' Very occasionally the subject would be mentioned, usually at the end of a long conversation. The greengrocer's wife would say:

'It's a crying shame, it is.'

'Oh, he's a dear little boy, and there are more terrible things in the world today.'

'My dear, a truer word was never said.'

Yes, the time we lived in then reduced our problem to its proper proportions.

Each year mother moved to the cottage in the country earlier in the year. She was fond of the apartment in town, but the fresh air was good for the children, and the almost inaccessible spot by the lakeside was a safe retreat in war-time for the father and many of their friends and relations.

In the spring of 1943 Jan's sister showed signs of

becoming a precocious young thing, which gave their mother moments of anxiety. But her fears were unfounded; Jan taught his sister manners in the most Christian way possible. As soon as she could crawl, and that was very soon, she upset all his games. If he sat playing quietly with a car, she would snatch it from him. He would watch her for a moment, turn around, take another toy from the cupboard and start playing with that without taking any notice of her. But she had other ideas. She would wriggle up to him and wrench the new toy from his hands. Philosophically, Jan would take up the original motor car and push it gently over the mat. This was the ideal way of curing his sister of her whims. In a very short time they were playing together harmoniously and have done so ever since.

Father and mother read everything they could lay their hands on about mongolism and they arrived at the following conclusions. According to the literature on the subject, the I.Q. of a mongoloid child is somewhere between 40 and 45; since Jan could therefore be assumed to be in the neighborhood of 50, it was reasonable to expect him to behave like a child of half his age. And that meant that for the time being they could set the same standard for him and for his younger sister, especially regarding what they were and were not allowed to do. On that point Jan was even a help, for he accepted discipline and had a fitting sense of right and wrong.

A Special Gift

It is a great mistake to misuse the prolonged babyhood of mongoloid children by spoiling them, since the effects of spoiling can seldom be eradicated. It is definitely *easy* to teach these children rules of good behavior, because they thrive on praise. From an early age Jan always tidied up, first his playpen and later the toy cupboard. Of course his mother was glad that she did not have to do it, and he was so happy and proud at being praised that the habit was formed for life.

That summer he began to talk. His first word was 'Heit' (the Friesian for father), which he practiced day-in day-out in the orchard, making his father as proud as a peacock. The other children were to follow his example, and later 'Heit' and 'Mem' became family usage. Jan added 'Mem' to his monosyllabic repertoire a whole month after he had learned to say 'Heit.'

His sister did not lag far behind, but when, at the age of eight months, she unexpectedly caught scarlet fever (there was an epidemic at the time), Jan Maarten was able to forge ahead again. Shortly afterward, however, he had a setback which almost cost him his life. His mother also came down with scarlet fever and his father recovered from a severe attack of quinsy just in time to discover a red mark on his son's body that made him suspect erysipelas. The village doctor, who was doing a superhuman job visiting his many scattered patients on a bicycle, confirmed the suspicion, and together they saved the sick child. A friend with nursing experience came to look after the mother and daughter. At last, when everyone had recovered, the family returned to town, profoundly grateful that they had survived this ordeal.

During the winter the problem of Jan's restless nights became more acute. He would roll to the edge of his crib in his sleep and thump his head rhythmically against the wooden side for hours on end. At the same time he would kick aside his blankets and so caught cold time and again. His mother and father were both sound sleepers. They did not mind getting out of bed several times a night to cover up their little son, but in the long run it exhausted them. The pediatrician considered this a clear indication that the time had come to find a suitable home for Jan Maarten. Apart from prescribing sleeping pills, which made no difference at all, he was unable to help the parents. They were both tired from lack of sleep and did not want to make so momentous a decision until they felt physically capable of doing so. And so a nurse was engaged, for the first time in Jan's life, to sit with him at night for a few weeks. She had trained in psychiatric hospitals, and so in her eyes there was very little the matter with Jan. They took to each other immediately and she treated him as if he were a normal child. The parents were as relieved at this as they were at being able to have nights of unbroken rest again. When the nurse left after those few weeks, Jan missed her sorely. He sat despondently on her bed saying, 'Och, dillekie, och, dillekie.' This, his version of the word 'sister,' became her nickname when she returned to the family in the autumn; they had asked her to spend a fortnight with them toward the end of the summer holidays of 1944, for Jan had longed to see her again. A severe railway strike broke out during her stay, keeping her prisoner at the lakeside cottage even longer. And again it was her relaxed and friendly interest in all that Jan did that made her an ideal companion in the darkest winter of the war.

An inspired idea about Jan's sleeping arrangements brought relief to the whole family that summer. He was still thumping his head against the side of his crib, disturbing the whole household. Now the frame on which the mattress rested was tied to four ropes which were hung on four hooks in the ceiling. A fisherman friend made a net big enough to form four 'walls' around the mattress. Jan now swung a few inches from the floor in a modified version of a hammock and loved it. The first three nights he crept up to the bedhead in his sleep, but as there was nothing to hit his head against, he merely tumbled half an inch off the mattress and sat in the net, his head still on his pillow, fast asleep. After that he no longer crawled out from under the blankets. He tried thumping his head in the pillow, which disturbed nobody, but that did not seem to afford him much satisfaction, and the habit gradually died a natural death. Jan slept in this hammock for nearly fifteen months. His parents screwed hooks into the ceiling of every room in the house so that the hammock could be moved as required. This was a great advantage at a time when the cottage had to be as elastic as possible, since men and women hiding from the Occupation Authorities were coming and going almost daily.

By the autumn of 1944 number three was well on the way. The baby, a boy, was born at the beginning of the blackest winter the country had known. He was welcomed by the whole family and Jan was a real big brother as he sat on a low stool holding the newcomer in his arms. As the winter drew on the baby had increasing difficulty in breathing. It was not easy to explain to the doctor what was worrying the father and mother and it was only when the fits occurred several times an hour that the doctor was able to diagnose something definite. There was no cure, and six months after his birth, Jan's brother passed away. When mother had laid the baby in his crib for the last time, she walked back slowly to the other children. Jan came to meet her and his grief seemed almost adult. As his mother knelt down in front of him, he took her head in his hands, gazed into her face and laid her head gently on his shoulder:

'Och, memmekie, och, memmekie,' his deep little voice consoled.

From now on Jan Maarten's mother and father were convinced that his intelligence quotient of barely 50 was more than compensated for by a 'quotient' of the heart far above average.

4

Going to School

THE end of the war in May 1945 left much sorrow in our little village. Many people had died, whose passing is still commemorated annually and for whom we still mourn. The German army retreated past the peaceful cottage for days and nights on end, while the children ran repeatedly to the bridge to watch all these men passing by.

A small cousin was, for a while, the youngest child in the house. She had been roaming with her parents from place to place, for they had been unable to stay in their home after the railway strike. She joined the family at the cottage in the spring. The house was rather full, as usual, and Jan was good and happy with so much going on around him. His speech improved, but at a much slower rate than that of his sister.

What were the parents to do when he got angry or was disobedient? They fully agreed with each other that he should not be slapped. He was exceptionally strong and should on no account be punished in a manner he might be tempted to try out on his little sister. Words of praise and words of warning influenced his behavior most effectively, but what words of warning were to be used now that the slap was to be a thing of the past? The next corrective measure to be introduced was the cold-water tap. At five Jan was still small and light enough to be carried swiftly to the nearest tap and have his head held under it if the situation so required. The treatment astonished him but also seemed to release some tension in him. A few drops of water on his flaxen hair were soon enough to convince him that he was heading in the wrong direction.

Jan's father and mother were now faced with decisions that were to affect the rest of their lives. His father started a new job and they decided to live permanently in the country. A cottage in the country and an apartment in town were a luxury they could no longer permit themselves, with so many houses destroyed in the war. At first the mother was upset by the thought of living permanently in the mildewed, primitive surroundings which she had readily accepted in the last few years of the war. Two considerations, however, made her change her mind. The father had basically always been a country man, who discovered in the war how much he relaxed and enjoyed every free moment he could spend in the open air. And then every real step forward achieved by Jan seemed to be due to living in the country. Later on his mother came to love the countryside for itself.

Now that they had come to live permanently in the village, they were soon allocated a better and more solidly built house. There, in the midst of paint-pots and ladders, 'Heit' and 'Mem' celebrated their 'pewter' wedding anniversary (a Dutch tradition), remembering the six and a quarter years of unforgettable experiences and rejoicing that they had arrived, safely so far, in the harbor of peace.

Jan and his sister 'sailed' through the empty house on a wooden tray. Heit and Mem toasted each other in tea, and the festive biscuits lay on pewter plates. There was a beautiful view over the lakes from the big window in the living room.

But what was Jan thinking of? He stood in the middle of the room, holding a wooden block in his hand in the inimitable way all boys have and all girls would like to have.

'Jan, don't throw that block.'

The tone of mother's voice left no room for doubt.

He looked at her triumphantly and threw with all his might. The block landed right in the middle of the irreplacable window-pane that trembled in its frame from the force of the blow, but miraculously survived the onslaught. Everyone was relieved, but what next? Mother marched up to Jan and took him firmly by the hand. He let himself be led off, realizing as he did that crime and punishment were inevitably linked. His mother thought hard and quickly as she propelled him out of the house; she had to think quickly of a suitable punishment for deliberate naughtiness that could be established as a precedent in the new house. As they reached the garage, her eye fell on the tap. As if this had been the sole object of the expedition, she held the boy with clothes and all under the jet of cold water. He did not utter a sound, but when she released him, he burst into tears and flung himself into her arms. They sat together, equally shocked, for a moment before mother fetched dry clothes for him. During the coming year, whenever he contemplated any naughtiness, one movement in the direction of the garage was usually enough to make him change his mind.

Shortly after the family moved, Jan's youngest sister was born. In the beginning neither he nor his other sister saw anything of the baby, since they were both suffering from a mild attack of whooping cough, which was fortunately immediately recognized as such by the doctor. The baby was kept quite separate from the other two.

That summer there were a number of things that kept him busy. Since the garden of the new house was bigger than that of the cottage, new toys were possible, such as a pedal car and a wooden scooter. Both were sources of endless pleasure. And then there was the wooden rocking-horse, which seemed to fulfil some need in the child. It was as if the pent-up energy that he had formerly expended in thumping his head against the side of his bed could now be released through his entire body in rhythmic rocking and singing. After a while either Mem or the nurse would distract his attention with something else, for fear of his going on too long, but a certain amount of rhythmic movement every day obviously did him good.

There was a lot of illness that summer: jaundice, inflammation of the middle ear, and quinsy attacked the whole family. Heit and Mem did not therefore immediately notice that Jan was growing moodier and moodier. His natural good temper and his chivalrous behavior toward his younger sisters and cousins were beginning to deteriorate. Soon, his parents realized that he was getting grumpy and obstinate, and they decided to keep an eye on him. Perhaps the time had come to seek admittance to a home?

This was the first time that the question had arisen seriously and the parents faced it squarely. They decided to consult their doctor on the advisability of taking him to a pediatrician or a child psychiatrist. It was essential that the other children should not suffer from any new development that might be taking place in Jan.

The doctor had become a good friend of the family and he gave Jan a check-up before committing himself. He found that the sturdy, apple-cheeked child was suffering from acute anemia: the hemoglobin content of his blood was down to forty-five.

'Oh, madam,' said the maid, 'no wonder the poor child is always crotchety.'

She was speaking from experience, for she too was anemic and was sometimes so tired she could hardly drag herself through the house.

It was not easy to help Jan over this obstacle, and anemia remained one of the weak spots in the frail armor of his health. Fortunately, his temper improved rapidly and he was soon his old sunny self again. For the first time his parents noticed a definite trait that manifested itself later time and again: whenever Jan was unhappy or moody, there was always something physically wrong and usually radically wrong at that. He did not give in readily and he wanted to be well and strong. He therefore never gave warning by being listless, but just suddenly caved in, at which point it was high time to do something about him.

It was fortunate that the anemia belonged to the past by the time Jan was old enough to go to school.

Although education was not compulsory for backward children in 1947, his father and mother agreed
that they should not delay in sending him, even
though he was still very babyish in his ways. They
first approached the Sisters of St. Ursula at Nieuwveen to inquire if they would consider taking a little
Protestant mongoloid child as a day-boy. This was a
novelty for the Sisters and they were not enthusias-
tic. During the parents' first visit, Sister Paula
showed them through the school, which she had
helped to found and from which she was about to
retire. She was obviously a woman of great practical
wisdom and warmth, and her advice to the disap-
pointed parents was that they should come back in a
month's time with Jan.

'It is an unusual and therefore difficult case for
Mother Superior,' she explained. 'She must be
allowed plenty of time to make up her mind.'

A month later father, mother and Jan presented
themselves at the convent a second time. They were
not very hopeful, but the intensely loving and happy
atmosphere of the convent had made such a deep
impression on them that they felt they had to try
again, even if their journey was to be in vain. They
sat anxiously in the waiting room, where the
sunlight was tempered by the tall, ancient trees in
the sheltered garden outside. The door opened to
admit Sister Eugenia, the school's secretary. Jan

Maarten ran up to her on his chubby little legs and grasped the full black skirts of her habit. He was intrigued by this new phenomenon in his life.

'Mem,' he asked, 'what kind of a man is this?'

Heit and Mem felt like children who'd committed some dreadful *faux pas*, but Sister Eugenia's eyes were smiling. She mentioned the long waiting-list for the boarding-school and spoke about the many children then attending the school who did not really belong there.

'We are really a teaching order,' she explained, 'not a nursing order. During the war we accepted many children whom we knew were incapable of being taught anything. But we had to hide them from the Germans, who fortunately never came here. And of course we can't now suddenly turn away those little ones who are patients.'

Father pleaded at this point that Jan would be present in class only, that he would be brought to school every day and fetched again and that he would not be taking another child's place in the boarding establishment. His arguments carried noticeably more weight than on the previous occasion. Sister Eugenia retired to consult Mother Superior. She stayed away a long time and came back shaking her head. The parents prepared themselves for a disappointment; who better than they were aware of the difficulties?

'Mother Superior is not sure whether to accept your proposal definitely,' said Sister Eugenia.

'She feels we should try it out until Christmas and then we can both see if the arrangement works.'

And so began a period of nine years in Jan Maarten's life which was of inestimable value for him and for the whole family.

5

God's Fairest Flowers

IT is impossible to tell the story of Jan's schooldays without first uttering heartfelt thanks to the Sisters whom we came to know at St. Ursula's, Nieuwveen. What a remarkable group of dedicated women! There was not one of whom we could not say, 'This is the right woman in the right place.' And the joy with which they carried out each task! When Mem made some remark about the class of mongoloid children to Jan's first teacher, she looked at her openly and cheerfully.

'Do you know, Mrs. de Vries, it is a privilege for us to work among these children. They are God's fairest flowers.'

And the Sisters accepted this privilege naturally and gladly and effortlessly.

The first time Jan's sister went with her mother to fetch him from school, Sister Miriam knelt down in front of her and said from the fullness of her heart, 'You almost forget here that they can look like this. Mrs. de Vries, how beautiful children are, like angels.'

But she stood up again almost immediately and returned cheerfully to her 'fairest flowers.'

A Special Gift

During the time Jan spent there, St. Ursula's had several different Mothers Superior, but Sister Eugenia saw him all the way through. He had four excellent teachers and there was always a fifth sister in the background who supervised the meals and breaks with true motherly devotion.

The value of these harmonious surroundings to Jan and the other mongoloid children at Nieuwveen was incalculable. And the parents of these children are wholly convinced that the Sisters of St. Ursula will in due time be rewarded by their Maker.

Jan Maarten started school in September, 1947. Four days a week he was on the road along the River Amstel to Nieuwveen before eight in the morning, early enough to enable his sister to be taken to infant school afterward. He was home by a quarter to five in the afternoon. He stayed at home on Wednesdays, for his mother was afraid that the long days might prove too much for him. There was no school on Saturdays.

In the beginning the new venture seemed to be an unqualified success, but difficulties arose before long. He went through stages of kicking, pricking people with pins and screaming, which could always be traced to a new arrival in the class who had behaved in this way.

'Oh, Mrs. de Vries, when that happens you have

58

them all kicking within a week,' said Sister Miriam.

For weeks on end Jan pretended he could not walk and lurched from the wall to the nearest chair in a masterly fashion. The urge to imitate and the virtuosity with which he expressed this urge were the source of both his progress and his misbehavior. He came to accept discipline more readily, but he also began to grow aware of his own wishes.

This was the beginning of a remarkable period. He would be playing and the time would come for him to tidy up. But Jan did not want to stop his game.

'All right, Jan, I'll wait.'

The grown-up concerned then stood obviously waiting. He could not bear the tension that this created and gave in sooner or later; in fact, he found it terrible. He often said, 'No, don't wait, I'll come now,' which he did indeed do. This waiting became the next disciplinary measure and one that was a strain to both mother and child. It was another aid in the process of learning to obey, but one that could not be used indiscriminately. With every new discovery in the sphere of discipline there was always the danger of it being used too frequently, or for unimportant reasons, not so much by the parents as by the other members of the household, who wanted to see if it really worked. Mother made a habit of discussing such matters with the younger children, sometimes forbidding them to interfere. Something that meant punishment for Jan as a person could not be allowed to deteriorate into a game. At the end of his first school year the parents discussed with the Sisters the difficulties that were arising at home through Jan's imitating new pupils. After much thought it was decided to move him to a class that was really rather above his standard, but at least he stopped acquiring bad habits. Now, the Sisters had always said that when a child was placed in a new class it took him about a year to get used to a new teacher, and only when he had done so would he start making progress again. But Jan Maarten did not advance even after the first year; the class really was too difficult for him.

There were other important events in his life during this period. He had always liked parties and outings and particularly enjoyed a visit to the fair. There he discovered his ideal in the shape of a small bicycle on a merry-go-round on which he was allowed to ride for a long time for about a penny. This experience inspired him with a great longing for a real bicycle. He did not often want something badly, but when he did, there was no getting him to change his mind.

His father's first comparatively long trip abroad took place in 1947. On the day of his return, as soon as he had been welcomed, Jan took his hand and asked, 'May I go for a drive with you?' Heit was surprised at his asking but pleased that Jan should show this initiative, and he promised to take him for a ride round the block before dinner. Jan appeared to have a definite purpose in mind. He wanted to go to a certain garage near the house of some friends of the family, a garage his father occasionally used. In the window was a green model jeep. When they arrived home with this, Mem was speechless.

'Did he ask for it?' she inquired incredulously, for Jan never asked for anything for himself.

'No,' replied Heit. 'He just told me I had to pay for it!'

Two years passed by and Jan was still obsessed by the idea of the bicycle he had ridden at the fair. His obsession was like a latent disease that keeps recurring. The family spent the month of June at the seaside. At the beginning of the village there was a bicycle shop, and mother had to make a detour whenever they went to the beach, for Jan could not be enticed away from the shop window in which 'his' bicycle was displayed. When asked what he wanted for his birthday, he could list only three things: a bicycle, crayons, and peppermints. Father and mother gave way and decided to buy a strong children's bicycle.

'After all, the girls can use it later,' they said.

'He'll be proud just to walk next to it holding the handlebars, as he did with the scooter at first.'

Little could they guess what would happen.

On October 22 he wheeled his new bicycle outside in a state of trance, mounted it and rode off down the garden path. The only thing he found difficult was dismounting, so the parents placed up-turned crates all over the garden, and that solved the problem. It was the first toy he did not willingly share with his sister. He allowed her to have a ride, but always stood waiting to take possession of his property again. For the first time something really belonged to him. No one grudged him the sole ownership of this long-coveted new toy, but he was encouraged to be 'noble' about letting others have a turn at riding it.

There was a steady stream of visitors to the house by the lake-side and Jan soon learned to be a good host.

'Shall I take your coat? Would you like a cup of tea? Do sit down, I'll go and call Mem.'

His naturally friendly disposition prompted this politeness, and he liked to make his contribution to the pleasant atmosphere in the home. Perhaps that was the motive for his obedience, which always had a beneficial effect on the younger guests. On the other hand, he learned a great deal from being treated like one of the others. When his father showed a film he had made on one of his trips abroad and the adults occupied all the available chairs, a single clear command:

'Children onto the floor—get a move on, Jan Maarten, you too!' was enough to make him take his place among the other youngsters.

The simplest solution to a problem is usually the most obvious one, and we discovered this when the problem of Jan's restlessness at night arose. He had always slept very restlessly; he would kick aside the covers in his sleep and consequently catch cold. He then had to be nursed back to health and the process started all over again. This had worried his nurse for some time, and when the family moved to the new house directly after the war, she asked for a large double bed for herself and Jan; she would then immediately be able to take action if he lay uncovered. That was a tremendous improvement, but Mem could not help feeling that it was the wrong solution and one that could not be permanent. After long deliberation, the simple idea of making a sleeping bag was born. It consisted of a very roomy bag made of two blankets pleated at the top and sewed to a strip of strong linen onto which an inner bag of sheeting could be sewed. The top of the bag could also be loosely drawn together by means of four pairs of strings. The sleeping bag was tried out during a seaside holiday and served its purpose admirably.

Once it came into use, Jan no longer caught cold at night.

In the spring of 1950 Mem discussed a new plan with the Sisters at St. Ursula's. Once a month Jan's nurse was allowed to spend a day at school. She helped the Sister in the class and followed her methods closely. The same books and teaching aids were bought, and from then on Jan was able to work at home with his nurse with the same material and in the same way as at school. Every day he was away from school he spent an hour doing lessons and so at last began to make gradual progress. *He learned to read and write and to count up to ten.* The Sisters attached great importance to the children's being able to count, since this was a great help later when they started handicraft lessons.

'If they can't tell the difference between two and three threads, there is so little they can be taught.' The following year he had no trouble at all in learning to tell the time. He was always surprising his parents and teachers in this way, as indeed many children at St. Ursula's did.

His visit to the fair had another positive consequence for Jan: he found a friend there. This boy was six months older than Jan and the second youngest child in a family living on a farm nearby. His father and mother had been very unfortunate in the beginning. There was nobody to explain why their little boy was different from other children, and they tried all sorts of remedies before someone had the courage to point out that this was not an illness that could be cured. It is particularly difficult to accept this truth about one of your children when the way to its revelation has been paved with broken hopes. The boy was nine when he started going to school with Jan. He was a healthy child and much more robust than Jan. He learned to do raffia work perfectly, but he never learned to read and write, for he started school three years after Jan did. He is now happily employed on his father's farm. Is illiteracy such a great handicap for mongoloid children, then? Yes, it certainly is. They derive such tremendous enjoyment from reading the newspaper for themselves; Jan Maarten's favorite topics were the Royal Family and the weather forecast. It gives them great pleasure to be able to write to friends and relations. The course leading to these great sources of pleasure must be embarked upon in good time, and in good time means when the child is about five or six years old. One of the Sisters at St. Ursula's explained why a delay is fatal.

'Our children need the whole of the first year and sometimes the second too to learn to work in a class and to listen to their teacher. *Every year that they are allowed to do as they like at home is doubly lost because it is very difficult to wean them from bad habits.*'

Jan and his friend now went to school together, usually singing. Jan knew a great many songs, but his friend's repertoire was much smaller. They did not need to express their affection for each other in words.

There was almost always something not quite in order with Jan Maarten's health. At this stage it was the 'snake's tongue' with which he had been born and which had grown as he grew. It had always been too big for his mouth and there was a lump on the tip which was gradually getting bigger. Jan was paying regular visits to an orthodontist in Utrecht at this time, and it was he who advised the parents to consult a surgeon about the abnormally long tongue. He did not mince his words.

'If he were my child I would operate on him tomorrow. Of course it is painful, but a tongue heals quickly and it's all over in a fortnight.'

Jan and his mother went to the hospital together for the first time. Mother was allowed to sleep with him and to do most of the nursing herself after receiving instructions on what to do. She installed a little bit of home in the hospital room.

The operation was painful and the first few days were difficult. But Jan's faith in mankind in general and in doctors in particular was unshaken. One of the stitches worked loose and it was evident that something would have to be done about it. With a heavy heart mother took her small son to the surgeon again. As soon as he entered the room Jan got up, took his hand and explained what had happened.

'My tongue isn't quite right. You may do it over again. I'll sit quite still and they needn't hold me down.'

They came back together after a while, Jan striding along like a man.

'I hope that will do the trick,' said the doctor.

'But remember, Jan Maarten, no hard things like peppermints and so on, or it'll open up again. Stick to porridge for the time being.'

Jan nodded earnestly.

'And ice-cream?' he asked.

The doctor burst out laughing.

'Tell your mother you deserve a nice big one.'

Jan followed the doctor's instructions in an exemplary manner ard the tongue healed beautifully.

This made all the difference to him. At home he was taught some deep-breathing exercises and at school he received speech lessons, thanks to the enterprising spirit of Sister Amelberga. A speech therapist had just been appointed at St. Ursula's to help the mongoloid children who had not yet learned to talk. The history of his appointment was interesting. It was believed at that time that a mongoloid child who had not begun to talk before his tenth year would never learn. A young speech therapist decided to test this out. He took a child already above this age limit and taught him to speak within a year. It was typical of St. Ursula's that he was subsequently asked to join their staff. Sister Amelberga promptly proposed that Jan also be given speech lessons.

'I think it would do him a lot of good,' she said. 'He talks so explosively and he himself must find that unsatisfactory. And now that his tongue no longer hampers him . . .'

No, that obstacle had been removed, and Jan's speech soon improved.

He was full of jokes which he loved airing. On one occasion he was in the lavatory when he heard noises indicating that somebody was going out. Surely they wouldn't leave without him!

The lavatory door was flung open and out shot Jan. He gave himself a smack on the bottom and cried, 'You stay where you are, I'll send you back by mail.'

He got on excellently with his grandfather, who was fond of teasing his grandchildren. Jan's intelligent little sister was sometimes the victim of Grandpa's practical jokes, for she simply did not expect her bun to disappear from her plate while she was helpfully looking around the room for the little

bird Grandpa said was there. The whole situation puzzled her but not Jan. 'And what about the
other bird then, Grandpa?' he asked.

'What other bird?' asked Grandpa, surprised.

'The one in your hand with the bun,' he laughed
infectiously.

'You bad boy,' sighed Grandpa, but the little girl
glanced gratefully at her big brother.

Grandfather would frown when he saw Jan cross
himself after saying grace; his orthodox Calvinist
heart found it difficult to accept the Catholic
education his grandson was receiving. But when Jan
recited the Lord's Prayer calmly and faultlessly, he
was deeply moved, and expressed his appreciation in
words that breathed a truly tolerant spirit.

Mother Superior also had her problems concern-
ing her little Protestant pupil.

'May he attend scripture lessons, or would you
rather he left the class?' she asked Jan's parents
during one of their visits to St. Ursula's.

'Do you think he'll learn anything wrong?' replied
his father.

Mother Superior understood the joke.

'We'll do our best not to let that happen,' she
smiled.

A good while later Mother Superior wished to

demonstrate to Jan's parents that he was deriving real benefit from the lessons. Jan stood before her and she asked him in a friendly manner:

'Tell me, Jan Maarten, what has God given you?'

Jan racked his brains.

'A soul,' he answered solemnly.

An excellent answer, but Mother Superior was not yet satisfied. 'And what else?'

Jan Maarten thought again.

'Chocolate,' he replied in tones of gratitude.

In the summer of 1952 Jan obtained the swimming certificate of the Royal Netherlands Swimming Association. This was entirely due to the efforts of a tireless teacher who had coached him regularly during the summer of 1951. In 1952 one of her brothers assisted her and together they made a proficient swimmer out of Jan.

His first contact with the deep end of the swimming pool was unforgettable. His teacher's brother thought it high time that Jan start taking swimming seriously, for he always played around in the shallow end and could not be persuaded really to try. He always wore a bathing costume with shoulder straps so that he could be 'fished' out of the water if he got into difficulties; in fact, the swimming pool management insisted on this type of costume being worn by all non-swimmers.

The brother decided to try out an experiment with Jan. With the fishing rod in his hand in case of accidents, he called Jan to him and gave him a sudden push into the water when the boy was least expecting it. Jan surfaced and swam to the side in a rage. He climbed out while the brother waited, smiling and pleased at the success of his maneuver.

'May I have your rod?' asked Jan.

The brother handed it over without suspecting anything, and Jan bent down to lay it carefully on the ground. From his squatting position he suddenly tackled the unsuspecting young man, who landed with clothes and all in the water. Jan was radiant!

From that time on he was made to practice seriously. By praising him lavishly his clever teachers managed to keep him at it and to improve his performance gradually. And then, one very windy day, he took the test and passed. It was a triumph for all concerned. Jan was inordinately proud of his certificate and his parents were profoundly relieved that he could now venture near water without risk.

The following spring Jan and his sisters had their tonsils removed. Mother accompanied the children to the hospital and slept in Jan's room so that she could look after him as she had done when his tongue was operated upon. His sisters were put in the children's ward. The specialist who performed the operation said that Jan had been the easiest of the three to handle because he had cooperated with such complete trust. This was a memorable but unpleasant Whitsun for Heit and Mem, but all three children enjoyed themselves. Once his tonsils were removed Jan was at last rid of his chronic cold.

In the years that followed, the parents realized time and again just how delicate Jan was. When they looked back at this stage in his life, it seemed as if the tonsils had been removed at the last possible moment. They could not have risked the operation at a later stage. *Their inevitable conclusion was that one should never postpone for a handicapped child what is merely advisable for a normal one.*

That year mother spent a month at the seaside with the children. In an ideal cottage the same routine, which was enjoyed by everyone, was resumed every year; every morning they worked and played on the beach, every afternoon a nap was followed by a walk in the woods. Jan thoroughly enjoyed himself. He played ball and cycled with his sisters. He built sandcastles and paddled. His imagination was extraordinarily fertile. Every morning he came downstairs pretending to be a different person, sometimes a cousin, sometimes the waiter at the hotel where the family occasionally dined during the weekends when father was with them. He was very observant and could imitate surprisingly small details. Very often one glance was enough to reveal who he was pretending to be. Granny accompanied the family every year and got on famously with Jan when he was in these moods. They all had great fun together.

Mother was worried about the boy during this month and her anxiety increased as time went on. He seemed to have developed the habit of jerking his head compulsively. Was she imagining things?

Father noticed the queer twitch during his weekend visit, too, but they decided to postpone taking action since their doctor was away and the pediatrician was attending a conference abroad. The following week Mem by chance witnessed a little scene that was quite unlike Jan. He lost his balance while cycling, fell and then jumped up and kicked his bicycle with rage. His pink cheeks and the healthy color of the inside of his eyelids gave no indication of what was troubling him. A visit to the doctor confirmed that he was again suffering from anemia. Could that nervous jerk of the head be put down to the same cause? As soon as their good friend the pediatrician returned from Geneva they decided to consult him. He gave the problem careful consideration, and Heit and Mem were to remember this talk time and again in the coming year. The doctor discussed quite frankly the difficult stage Jan was now approaching. He was a frail craft to keep afloat, and in the coming years the sea of life would be rough and stormy for him. The physical changes about to take place were not likely to be typical of a normal adolescence, though that *could* happen. But his resistance to illness would be greatly lowered and every minor ailment could have grave consequences.

'A doctor can't keep an eye on him for you; after all, you yourselves are specialists in Jan,' warned their friend. 'Don't hesitate to call in medical advice immediately if anything threatens to go wrong; you owe it to him.'

A neurologist treated Jan Maarten for the twitch and the anemia was cured. He started growing now too and he lost his puppy fat.

That autumn there was an epidemic of a mild type of jaundice, and Jan Maarten was one of the victims—fortunately, for the strict diet, without fat and rich in protein, completely cured the chronic stomach ache of which he had complained ever since he could talk. He was inordinately pleased and relieved at this, which made him a much easier patient than his sisters, who had to be coaxed gently over their jaundice depression.

This was the period in which Jan no longer needed a nurse. Once the anemia was a thing of the past, he slept much more peacefully, and the success of the sleeping bag meant that he did not have to be watched so carefully at night. In 1950 he had moved into a bedroom next to that of this parents, who could now keep an eye on him at night without losing too much sleep themselves.

Mem now accompanied Jan to St. Ursula's once a month. She learned a great deal there and her memories of those days will remain with her all her life. The geography lesson was one such memorable occasion. Jan was undoubtedly the best pupil in this class, since all those strange names meant something to him.

The children were learning the five continents.

'Who knows the name of one of the continents?'

'Europe,' answered the class in unison.

'Good. And another one?'

Jan raised his hand.

'America. Heit has been there.'

'Good. Try again.'

'Australia. Heit and Mem have been there.' And he proudly showed the class his koala bear. Africa, Asia, Jan had heard of them all, had received letters and picture postcards from all over the world. Then Europe was dealt with and the class had their say again.

'Spain, that's where Sinterklaas * lives; Italy is where the Pope lives.'

* Sinterklaas, or St. Nicholas, is to Dutch children what Santa Claus is to the English-speaking world; his traditional home is Spain.

A Special Gift

Jan Maarten was able to make his contribution here, too, happily and proudly, though he was sometimes too bold.

'The Netherlands is divided into eleven pieces. You all know that, don't you? Now what do we call those pieces?'

The class was silent. What *do* we call those pieces?

Jan raised his hand.

'Proverbs,' he ventured.

Later he and his mother practiced the word 'province' over and over again; it was a much more abstract conception than the Spain of Sinterklaas.

Among the children at St. Ursula's were also a number from broken homes. As Sinterklaas festivities approached (they are held on December 5), mother discussed these children with one of the Sisters with a view to providing any little extras that might be needed.

'Are there also mongoloid children in your wards?' she asked.

'No,' was the reply. 'Mongoloid children don't live to be six under such circumstances.'

This reminded Jan's mother yet again how delicate mongoloid children are, even when they are born with a sound heart. Many of them have heart defects. Either way, they need loving care at every stage of their lives.

* *

76

In the spring of 1954 a very special event took place. Jan, his sisters, Heit and Mem all went on a holiday to Juan-les-Pins on the French Riviera. It was a wonderful experience. They almost filled the little *pension*. Jan's behavior was exemplary; he was always polite, always thrilled with everything. His good ear enabled him to imitate French words and phrases faultlessly, and he enjoyed running errands and saying a pleasant word to the waiter or to the elderly guests. When either of his sisters looked at her plate in disgust, Heit and Mem were able to keep in the background.

'Mmm, jolly good,' Jan Maarten would say.

'Merci, monsieur'—that was to the waiter.

'Shall I eat your helping?'

No, she would rather just taste it herself, and then the enthusiasm would become general.

His reaction to the completely different surroundings was remarkably adult. The family usually spent the mornings on the beach and the afternoons up in the beautiful countryside of the French Riviera. During a picnic in the snow Jan sat quietly looking about him after grace had been said. The mountains rose white and majestic all round the little valley.

'On mountains and in valleys . . .' he murmured, quoting from a well-known Dutch hymn. 'So God is here too.'

The family drove back home through a countryside in bloom. The weather was fine, the plum trees covered in pale pink blossom, and the children could not stop singing.

'You must stop for half an hour, children, you'll all be hoarse.'

So they played 'I spy with my little eye' for half an hour and then burst into song again.

Evening fell sooner than Heit expected. The children were drooping. There on the hill before them was the Château St. Jean, now a hotel. Yes, they could get rooms there, one for Heit and Mem with a room leading off it for Jan and one for the girls on the other side. It was too good to refuse, and nobody regretted the extra luxury. It was like a fairy-tale. In the impressive dining-hall, where the walls were covered with tapestry, the youngest child sat at table with her hands tucked under her.

'You mustn't do that in a posh hotel,' admonished Mem.

'I can't help it, Mem, I'll crumple up if I don't.'

Jan found it all wonderful . . . the high rooms, the chandelier, the food. After dinner Mem bathed him quickly and put him to bed. Lying in the enormous Louis XV bed, he put his arms around her neck and murmured the beginning of an evening prayer, but before he had recited the first line he was fast asleep.

He won many hearts during the trip through France. There are more mongoloid children in France than in Holland but they are seldom seen.

Hardly a day passed without his parents being approached by a stranger.

'Ah, Madame, my eldest son is just like yours,' and then came the question and the sorrow.

'But how, but how is your boy so much more advanced than mine . . .'

No, Jan is not much better, he is an 'average' mongoloid child. Mother realized that at St. Ursula's. But Jan Maarten's circumstances have resulted in the development of his great capacity to give and to receive love. That is why he is so valued a member of the family.

At the beginning of 1955 there were no omens of the catastrophe that was to befall Jan Maarten that year. He was now an industrious member of his weaving class and produced dusters, towels and table cloths under the tireless guidance of Sister Anselma. At home extra attention was paid to reading, writing and arithmetic. His elder sister was now attending a grammar school, the younger was still at primary school. Mem managed to teach a few hours a week again, much to her joy.

In spring Jan caught 'flu' which was followed by a mild infection of the kidneys. He bore the dullness of a saltless diet as bravely as always. The family again stayed at the little *pension* at Juan-les-Pins in April together with Grandmother and a friend of the eldest daughter. It was again a great success. To his sorrow, Jan was not allowed to bathe because of the kidney trouble, but a water bike compensated largely for the deprivation. And of course there were excursions by boat and by car. Jan joined in everything enthusiastically but tired quickly and liked to keep Grandmother company. He was quite well again in the summer. The lakeside house was always full of cousins and friends in the summer holidays. They came to learn sailing at the nearby sailing school and to pass the summer swimming, rowing and working in the garden. Jan was also allowed to take a course in sailing with his younger sister and a friend. He found it tiring but thoroughly enjoyed it and really did his best. He slept in the attic, in what might be called the 'guest dormitory,' with six other boys, who were all very kind and looked after him well. He grew taller and thinner.

At the end of August the family spent a week in Brabant. He was tired out from the first day. He dragged himself about, determined to enjoy himself, but it was evident that he was perpetually exhausted. His mother was terribly worried, but she could give no real reason for her anxiety. She took him to the doctor once or twice for minor upsets, but they were not serious in themselves. School was due to start on September 3, but before embarking on a new school year, his mother took him to their old friend, the family doctor, and repeated what she had said nine years ago:

'I want to see a specialist. There's something wrong and I don't know what.'

Their knowledgeable friend again first checked up before consulting a specialist, and again he discovered what was wrong in a very short time. Jan Maarten had diabetes and had to be admitted to the hospital immediately.

He was strangely precocious at this time.

'Do you think I'm going to die?' he asked a close friend of the family.

'But Jan Maarten, what makes you ask that?' she answered with tears in her eyes.

'Because I think I am,' he said calmly.

'Do you think Mary will come and fetch me?' he asked his mother the same evening.

'What would you do if she came?' his mother replied. She sat on the edge of his bed watching his face. She was to take him to the hospital the next day.

'I'd go with her,' said Jan, happily sure of himself.

'And what about me?' his mother asked involuntarily. She could have bitten out her tongue, but she felt singularly helpless and desolate.

'Yes, it wouldn't be nice for you, but I'd like so much to go,' he said longingly.

This is really the end of the history of what could be called a 'normal' mongoloid child. But fortunately Jan's history is not yet at an end. It was very difficult for his parents to accept the fact of his diabetes. He himself accepted every setback with such courage and with so little fuss as would put many adults to shame. He drew on reserves of natural cheerfulness and had complete faith and trust in what the adult world had in store for him. He accepted life as God gave it to him.

6

Venturing Further Afield

IN this chapter I shall try to emphasize what may be of interest to the parents of older mongoloid children. Of course, Jan Maarten's life has been bound up with the complication of his illness ever since September, 1955. But this in no way affected his potential, which was determined by the same factors as that of other mongoloid children.

Jan spent a month in the hospital with his mother. How many 'friends for life' he made there! How great was the help given by the specialist and the matron to his mother as she familiarized herself with the complex of new problems. And how many hearts did Jan not win as he tried to adapt himself to a new rhythm of life, quietly seeking distraction in weaving and jigsaw puzzles.

At home in October, he gradually returned to normal. His surprise that the doctor was again able to do away with all the unpleasantness was transformed into complete obedience to the new rules. He was able to go back to school in November. St.

Ursula's co-operated, as always, in superhuman fashion. Jan took his diet lunch with him every morning in a schoolbag, and the Sister whose task it was to prepare a midday meal for three hundred children found time to cook his meal too. A new watch helped him remind his teacher when it was time for his 10-o'clock snack or his afternoon drink. The regular rhythm of his life gradually established itself and his confidence began to return. But one great drawback manifested itself: his resistance to illness was greatly lowered, and whenever there was an outbreak of an infectious disease at school, Jan was sure to be the second child to catch it.

In January, 1956 a nurse again joined the family to ensure a measure of regularity in Jan Maarten's life in the midst of a busy household. The family's tempo could not be adapted to suit him; Heit's work was demanding and his hours irregular. The number of children in the house varied continually because there was always room in this lakeside haven when family complications occurred in town. Jan liked people and enjoyed having guests, whom he inevitably welcomed charmingly. But he himself could not be allowed to suffer neglect on their account. It was the none-too-easy task of the nurse to see that this did not happen.

The older boys who stayed in the house for shorter or longer periods were responsible for introducing quite naturally a new phase in the disciplinary side of Jan's upbringing. His observant eye and sensitivity to moods soon conveyed to him the purport of a 'talk' in Heit's study when Heit wished to 'discuss' certain sins of omission or commission.

'Must I come to your study?' he would ask anxiously when he realized he had done something quite wrong. Heit did not hesitate to seize these opportunities.

'Yes, you come along with me.'

A session in the study has been an effective disciplinary measure ever since.

Before the summer holidays began father and mother decided, in consultation with the Sisters at St. Ursula's, that Jan would not return to school in September. He was nearly sixteen by this time, and his frequent absences through illness were destroying the beneficial effect of working in the community of the classroom. Jan had spent nine years at St. Ursula's. In summer he had ridden along the beautiful River Amstel, in winter he had slithered along the winding, slippery polder roads. He had seen many alterations and improvements in the school but one thing remained constant and from that he benefited to the full: the loving, devoted, dedicated hearts of the Sisters of St. Ursula, who endeavor to recognize and stimulate each tiny talent the children assigned to their care may possess. *When conditions at home, whatever they may be, make it impossible to bring up a backward child with his brothers and sisters, he will most certainly be happy in the type of institution Jan Maarten was privileged to attend.* We in Holland are fortunate that so much is done for handicapped children and done so well.

Yet despite this, there are still a multitude of problems and cares, some of which do not crop up until the child is sixteen. Jan's father and mother had seldom made long-term plans for the little craft that rode so unsteadily on the waves. But they had departed from this principle, shortly before Jan was discovered to be diabetic, and they had looked about them to find out what would be best for him after his sixteenth birthday. Arrangements had just been made when he fell ill in August, 1955. He was to have attended an institution for older boys as a day-boy several days a week, for his parents were convinced of the desirability of his sharing duties and activities with boys of his own age. The diabetes changed these plans. It was evident that this frail craft needed a single person at the helm.

'Coming home' was no problem for Jan. His friend was also leaving school to help his father on the farm; Jan left school to help the gardener.

* *

Despite a certain amount of variety, we tried to adhere to a fairly regular timetable for Jan. After breakfast and with the help of the nurse he cleared the table and washed the dishes. These chores were followed by lessons in reading, writing, and arithmetic, as varied as possible, until 11 o'clock. After morning coffee he helped the gardener until lunch-time. Every afternoon he rested for an hour and then returned to the garden, but in winter the afternoons were devoted to weaving, rug-making or some other handicraft.

The nucleus at home to which he now belonged was not very big. Apart from Mem and the nurse, there was help in the house and in the garden. Every time there was a change of staff, the same conversation was held in a different form. *The medical friends of the family all agreed that Jan's adolescence need not be unduly problematic, provided he was not unnecessarily and wrongly stimulated. Jan loved jokes and innocent teasing, but playful fights were consciously avoided. Jan and other backward children are remarkably strong and it would be a dangerous mistake, and one that is all too often made, to allow them to try their strength unchecked in any way.*

And so his self-discipline was deliberately encouraged.

'But Jan Maarten, a gentleman doesn't do that.' He prided himself on his good manners and an appeal to them seldom failed. The whole household worked together to keep the ship on a straight course through the turbulent waters of adolescence.

A Special Gift

Jan had not been home long when Heit was obliged to go off on one of his long annual trips. The family never liked his being away, and Jan had a long talk with his father before he left that had remarkable consequences. Shortly before his departure, Heit came home with a big drum for his son.

'I promised him he could have it,' he said, somewhat apologetically, to his wife, who was nonplussed at this latest acquisition.

Jan's delight was so infectious that she soon made inquiries of the painter who played the big drum in the village brass band. Would it be possible for Jan to have lessons? Of course it would. The band's conductor soon paid a visit and so began the lessons that were to be the joy of Jan's life. Mem and the conductor felt their way in this unknown territory together. Jan had a good sense of rhythm and could soon beat a march and a waltz. But could he learn to count, could he be taught the value of notes? That went splendidly. But what about the quarter and eighth notes? Jan had done a great deal of arithmetic in his life but he had never managed to learn fractions. With no expectations whatsoever, the teachers broached the subject of 'One and two and, a one and a two and . . . ,' and it was immediately clear that they had been making a fuss for nothing, just as they had when he had learned to tell the time. He could not understand what they found problematic. Of course, two sixteenths make an eighth note, two eighths a quarter note; two halves are the same as one whole. Surely everybody knows *that!*

When he was allowed to practice with the village band a few months later, his joy knew no bounds. He made several devoted friends there who loved music as he did. They encouraged him and played easy pieces in which he could join. And he thoroughly enjoyed listening to other pieces that were too difficult for him to play.

Music is an inexhaustible source of pleasure in his life and the village band one aspect of that joy. Later on he learned to play the piano. Not much, of course, because he found it difficult, but he loved duets.

Not only did the conductor of the village band help him, the family music master also did much to develop his ear for music. He learned to listen more attentively to records and to radio programs. One day he was allowed to go to a concert in Amsterdam and stay until the intermission. He found it fascinating and talked about it for days.

Once he was given a set of triangles on which he could accompany other members of the family when they played the piano. He also accompanied the choir of angels at the carol service held in the village church at Christmas.

Another fixed item on Jan's weekly program was the handicraft lesson. Thanks to the tireless inventiveness of a close relation, there were always new objects for Jan Maarten to make. And how proudly he would give them away!

'I made this for you myself.'

'As long as the difficulties are purely organizational we shall not bypass them, but shall face them squarely.'

As the annual holiday approached, this time to be spent in Alassio on the Italian Riviera, the parents were reminded of their resolution of long ago. Was it still possible to go with the whole family? Was it not becoming too complicated? The nurse and Mem worked it out together, making lists of what would have to be taken with them and what substitutes could be found for Jan's diet. Once they sat down to it, they found a solution to every problem. Jan and his nurse accompanied the family.

During the first few days Mem helped with the arrangements, but before they realized it, everything was going smoothly. The hotel was given the diet list, the nurse kept an eye on things and was allowed to prepare what was needed in the kitchen at all times. The whole family thoroughly enjoyed the holiday. Jan's times quite often did not coincide with those of the hotel, but then the nurse saw to what was necessary. Finally, he often had his insulin injection during a hike in the mountains, or he would have his snack, at exactly the right time, standing on a platform in a cave by candlelight, watching the stalactite dripping away the time. He was very happy, sharing these experiences with the rest of the family.

The older he became the more he enjoyed our travels. His mother had noticed when he was quite small that he loved beautiful things. Encouraged by this, she had taken him to the Rijksmuseum in Amsterdam with his eldest sister. The first visit lasted only half an hour and they went back again later. They went to other exhibitions too, but always avoided long visits. These visits were also a source of pleasure, and Jan soon showed a preference for religious subjects. This interest of his was invaluable when the family went on holiday. He always accompanied them when they went to look at something beautiful and so he could, in his fashion, share their pleasure too.

One year, when the two girls were still at grammar school, the family decided to spend a holiday in Greece with a family of cousins. It was quite a large party that was to set out on this exciting expedition, and plans were discussed on many evenings. Jan sat quietly listening to the others. He himself looked at pictures of what he would be seeing in Greece with his nurse and he read a simple version of the story of the Trojan War. Once in Greece he happily recognized many of the objects he had 'studied' at home and inevitably raised his hand when the guide mentioned a familiar name. Thus the holiday was as unforgettable for him in his own way as for his sisters. He and Spiros, the chauffeur, who spoke only Greek, wept bitter tears on each other's shoulders when the time came to part. Jan had often sat next to Spiros, had laughed with him and sung with him. They had thumped each other cheerfully on the back, calling each other 'my friend.' They will not forget each other lightly.

Jan Maarten's ability to listen quietly and absorb what he was capable of understanding stood him in good stead in another important sphere. He liked to accompany the family to church, where his father often played the organ. He would sit quietly near him or go up into the gallery. He always listened attentively and joined in the singing during the services. A number of years were devoted to preparing him for confirmation. He read a children's Bible together with a minister and also discussed with him what he had read by himself. When there was family Bible reading at home he frequently recognized the passage as one he had read himself or had discussed with the minister. His prayers were always entirely sincere: he would fervently pray for the safe return of a relation away on a journey or the recovery of a sick friend. His trust in God was and is absolute. He was used to not understanding everything, but sure that his trust would not be betrayed. The minister and his parents agreed that Jan could teach them a great deal.

Apart from taking him to church, Heit also occasionally took Jan shooting or fishing. This happened only rarely, for both activities were rather too strenuous for the boy. But his pleasure in going out with the men was so great that the extra organization it required was well worthwhile. The experience of joining a shooting party and dining with the sportsmen afterward gave Jan a strangely manly air. He then, like some of the other guests, enjoyed making a speech in which there was a compliment or a word of comfort for everyone.

'Uncle . . . I still think you're a jolly good shot!'

The diabetes stayed relatively well under control for a number of years. Then dark clouds began to gather over Jan's head. Father and mother had always kept a careful eye on him ever since the illness had manifested itself. Relations in the medical profession and good friends had often helped to avoid trouble through their interest and advice. But there came a time when they too were powerless.

There was something treacherous undermining his strength. His twentieth birthday fell in a period of great weakness. When his friends of the village band came to bring him a morning serenade—which he had hoped against hope they would—he had to lie down every ten minutes because he was too exhausted to stay on his feet.

When Heit and Mem took him to the hospital in January they knew that the seas of life were beginning to swamp the frail craft. It was a miracle that the cause was discovered by an excellent specialist in time and a touch of genius gradually brought about a change in Jan's apparently hopeless condition.

He recovered very slowly, and this time he emerged from the clouds much more adult than ever before. Every past illness had been forgotten very soon. But he did not forget this one. It was a long time before he regained confidence in his health, but once he had, he was and remained deeply grateful.

A year later speech lessons were started again with the teacher who had first helped him at St. Ursula's. The lesson itself was only an hour a week, but he worked hard at it and soon made progress. Jan liked to welcome guests at table and his ability to express himself on these occasions improved noticeably.

Even when he was angry he was able to put his thoughts into words now. Mem noticed that one day when, sitting at his bedside, she scolded him for losing his temper unnecessarily about something he had misunderstood.

'And now I want to hear from you that you won't do it again,' she concluded.

It was very quiet in the little room. Mem sat calmly waiting while Jan leaned inexplicably obstinate, on his hand. It was so quiet that Mem peeped to see if her son had fallen asleep. But Jan was fighting a battle that every human being has to fight. His deep voice sounded like a sigh.

'Why don't you do as Mem asks? You know she's right!'

Again silence.

'I want to do it, I know she's right, but it's so difficult.'

Jan Maarten sometimes spontaneously expressed a wish which, when it was fulfilled, opened up prospects of pleasure that were undreamed of. One such instance occurred when the family was to celebrate a festive occasion while on holiday in a little Italian *pension*. Father and mother had bought presents for each other and for the girls.

'Is there anything you'd particularly like, Jan Maarten?'

'A camera,' he replied without a moment's hesitation.

His parents looked at each other in amazement. Jan had very weak eyes. The specially ground lenses of his spectacles were a great help, but everything to do with seeing had always cost tremendous concentration.

'Let's give him one,' his father said. 'After all, we asked him what he wanted and he was quite decided. Let's see if we can find something suitable.'

A shopping expedition to the village produced a simple camera that was easy to manage.

The celebrations took place at the foot of a small deserted chapel at San Bartolomeo. The whole family gazed at the beautiful view from the low walled terrace. The hills were covered with young green leaves and yellow broom. Far below was a small airfield from which tiny two-engined aircraft took off and landed like gulls. A picnic, a few speeches, the presents! Jan's pleasure was as intense as it had been when he was given a watch on his twelfth birthday. The family all took turns in helping him and the film was soon finished. They took it to be developed the same evening.

When he went to collect the snapshots he was so inordinately happy that the family could not but share in his joy. There was something on every snapshot, even though it was sometimes no more than a head! Taking photos with this simple camera became a hobby he practiced with great concentration. He did not mind being helped, but the photos he took by himself were certainly not the worst.

When it was suggested that his speech teacher should give him English lessons, Jan at first felt honored, but then said earnestly:

'I'm afraid I'll find it rather hard.'

'That doesn't matter, Jan Maarten; it's good to tackle something difficult.'

He wanted to sleep on it, and the next morning he had decided to take the plunge. After all, he would then be able to talk to our foreign guests. He worked hard at his lessons, learning a few phrases and odd words, helped by the fact that he usually understood most of what was said to him.

'May I bother you for a light?' he asked, daringly, an Australian guest, who promptly started telling him a long story. Nodding and smiling pleasantly as if he understood every word, he tactfully withdrew.

'Just a drop?' he asked another, handling the bottle like an experienced bartender.

'Thank you,' said the guest, taking Jan for granted. Jan filled his glass carefully, conscious of his responsibility.

The elocution and English lessons helped Jan's general development so that he still made progress. And then he was twenty-five years old. His twenty-fifth birthday was celebrated in grand style. He toasted his guests in wine and declared from the bottom of his heart:

'How glad I am that I'm at last twenty-five.'

There were certainly others who were quite as glad as he and grateful too. Heit and Mem remembered how he had been given only eight years to live. The decision to enjoy from day to day all the special sweetness this child had brought into their lives traced a golden thread through their memories of twenty-five years.

'What made him like this?' his mother asked herself as she watched him radiant among his guests. 'His heart of gold was a gift he brought into the world when he was born. We have been able to help him acquire the self-discipline which enabled him to overcome his tremendous physical handicaps. The unique place that is his in our small community is a gift from God to us all, for which we can never be grateful enough.'

And Heit put his feelings into the words of the prayer of thanks with which he closed this memorable day:

'Help us to live with our cares and with our blessings.'

7

A Special Gift

THE gift of being able to observe quietly and imitate accurately brought Jan much farther in life than was generally thought possible. In this book I have tried to record Jan's progress through life insofar as it might be of interest to other parents. Not that I would wish them to 'imitate.' How utterly impossible it would be to equate one very special case with another. But I have tried to give examples of certain rules which helped us and which helped to create for our son that atmosphere of security in which he was able to develop his limited mental powers and the generous gifts of his heart.

Children like Jan Maarten will in the first place demand of us that we accept them as they are. If we really wish them to share in our family life in a harmonious fashion and still be themselves, they must be accorded a status comparable to that of the other children in every way, including the performance of tasks and the acceptance of discipline. We found our decision to demand of him what we would have of a child of half his age entirely justified and practicable. Of course this is not the only way. But it is important to mark out a clearly defined path that is also acceptable for the other children in the family.

Having chosen a reasonable framework, let us not expect our other children or ourselves to act in a 'special' way. The more 'normal' our behavior and attitude to the child, the easier it is for the outside world to accept him and relax in his presence. Once a Jan Maarten is given his niche in the family, he will require more vigilance and greater attention than a normal child. We never forgot the warning 'These children are delicate.' They *are* delicate, they often react differently from other children, but that does not necessarily mean that this fact must be blindly accepted. Jan was privileged in that the doctor who attended him most frequently was a village doctor who was not easily discouraged.

People are much too apt to generalize about mongoloid children and to say that

> they all have a chapped skin,
> they all have perpetual colds,
> they all have pimples and sores, and
> they all have inflamed eyes.

And these are only a few of the remarks to which I

object. For their skin is tender, but if their faces are washed with water only once a day and for the rest cleaned with a good cleansing cream, the roughness disappears for good in a short time.

Jan did have a perpetual cold until his tonsils were removed and we left that stage behind. Cuts are inclined to become infected very soon, and an ointment that draws out the inflammation should always be kept at hand. *If we accustom ourselves to treating every smallest threat with attention, we can prevent many tiresome infections.*

The same applies to the eyes. A good eyewash and ointment should always be in the medicine cabinet. We should learn how to use both properly and use them regularly—throw away every swab immediately after use and always wipe toward the nose. It is no trouble at all to add these medicaments to your first-aid kit. There are so many small, almost professional 'tricks of the trade' a mother should know for any child, but especially for these children.

Regular medical check-ups are essential too. And it is a good thing to mention to the doctor everything that seems at all strange in the child's behavior.

The development of a retarded child's restricted mental powers requires our devoted care too. It is wise to read extensively on the subject, but it is certainly not necessary to discover everything oneself. Such children observe carefully and imitate well. Abstract ideas are not their strong point. They find it difficult to grasp ideas like 'more,' 'less,' 'bigger' and 'formerly.' When they learn something new, they must be helped with great patience to practice it and be praised enthusiastically for every sign of progress. At first every single skill costs tremendous effort, but once they have mastered it, they retain the knowledge and constant practice makes it familiar. They are proud of their achievements.

Their ability to learn new skills, to make progress, continues for a long time. Today more and more is being done with mongoloid children over sixteen, for even then they are still capable of learning. They derive so much pleasure from making something they can give away that it is really worthwhile teaching them to weave, make rugs or some other handicraft. They are constructive and enjoy being creatively busy. That is why they can become so useful about the house. They enjoy helping father or mother with such daily chores as they can manage, and they do them carefully and precisely.

The special gift of their warm hearts requires the utmost vigilance from those who are privileged to guide their steps along the path of life. I repeat: it is essential to know what you want and to lay down simple, hard and fast rules, for it is thus that these children are given the security they need for their development in every respect. Their ability to distinguish between right and wrong is quite normal and that is a great help. Their natural goodness of heart has free play. They are prepared to do a great deal for others provided they are not spoiled. They respond like flowers in the sun to a word of praise and are quickly upset by disapproval; on the whole they are particularly sensitive to the moods of others.

If one of the family does something wrong, Jan promptly takes the blame.

'We broke a cup [or forgot a message]. Are you cross with us?'

He cannot bear leaving anyone in the lurch. We must handle these tender consciences with great care. We must not be afraid of making mistakes but we must acknowledge having made them and act differently next time.

'It is difficult to cure these children of bad habits,' one of Jan's teachers once said. It is our task to teach them good ones, both for their sakes and for ours.

These children are particularly receptive to religious instruction. Again, it is only devoted care that produces the best results, and these results are really extraordinary sometimes. There is much we can learn from Jan and his brothers and sisters. The two ministers who prepared Jan for confirmation agreed with us wholly on that point.

Jan was confirmed one Easter and his confirmation was a highlight in his life and in that of the whole family. His preparation had started months beforehand under the guidance of a devoted minister who never condescended to him and was always struck by Jan's ready acceptance of the message the Scriptures convey.

During the service his 'Yes' rang out loud and clear. The minister, deeply moved, addressed a few words to Jan, who stood in the church, a radiant and wholly worthy child of God.

Is it necessary at the end of this book to mention that material circumstances do not play the chief part in the development of a backward child? What is important is the atmosphere of peace and security with which we surround him, the attention and devoted care we are prepared to give to this 'dearest child of God.' Then, in whatever walk of life he may have been born, there is every likelihood of his growing up to be a happiness to those closest to him, even though a stranger often sees him only as an object of care and pity.

The Book of Proverbs teaches us:

A Special Gift

'The heart knoweth his own bitterness; and a stranger doth not intermeddle with his joy.'

The whole of our situation is summarized in these wise words from the distant past. As parents of backward children, we know the bitterness of taking a subnormal child in our arms and to our heart. A very personal, intimate joy can accompany that bitterness on the child's progress through life.

This book was written to bear witness to that joy.

Epilogue

BUT now his voyage is over. Life was not easy for Jan during those two last years. Slowly at first, but nonetheless surely, the vitality he once had ebbed away. There was a grave crisis, eighteen months before the end, from which he recovered to some extent. A strict diet combined with various medicines managed to keep his health in precarious balance. He continued to busy himself with the activities that remained to him and from which he derived such pleasure: his music, his speech-training lessons, writing birthday letters to his many friends, simple handicrafts, paying visits.

He had one great desire at that time and that was to accompany the family to Scotland, where they had already spent several happy holidays. His wish was granted after much thought and preparation. He had many months of quiet enjoyment with his Scottish friends: half an hour's sea-fishing—and he always came home with a respectable catch!—a short walk to feed the pheasants, a chat using the few words of English he knew. We were all most painfully aware of the unique quality of these days.

The little complications that had always been

part of his life had now become threats that were ever more difficult to ward off. We, who all loved him so, deeply felt our growing helplessness and knew that it could not go on like this.

He himself always wanted to spare our feelings. 'How are you feeling, Jan Maarten?'

'Oh fine, thanks.'

The words were like a sigh in those last weeks. 'You never complain, do you, my boy?' exclaimed his old friend, the specialist. Jan glanced at him attentively. 'How is your wife?' he asked, interested as always in the well-being of others.

'What shall we read this evening, Jan Maarten?' his father asked on one of the last days.

'Psalm Twenty-Three, Heit,' and father read, 'The Lord is my shepherd, I shall not want.'

When we think of Jan Maarten now, the heart reacts differently from the mind. We remember how, when he left school, we sought ways of providing activities that he could carry out at home. Afterward we should have to try to settle his future in some other way, should he survive us. We knew the moment would come when we would have to entrust him to the care of other people. So many parents have to face this problem as their handicapped children grow up. The parting is difficult even when one thinks one has found the best solution, and the vigilant guidance required afterwards is time-consuming and often heartbreaking.

Because Jan fell ill we were spared these problems. For more than twelve years he lived at home, a working, active, irreplaceable member of the family. Irreplaceable—yes, and then the memories come crowding in. All our friends make their contribution to our rich store, for almost each one of them can tell of some specific happening or expression that struck them as being typical of Jan and which they will always associate with him. Irreplaceable—this word, and all these memories, touch the heart which knows its own sorrows. How did Jan always manage to transform our grief and to put us on the track of 'being happy together' in such unexpected ways? With his limited mental capacities and his great heart he had all that is really essential to human happiness. His special way of looking at people and things meant so much to us that our daily life now seems almost colorless without him.

He lived in *our* world insofar as he was able. But the miracle was that he opened up *his* world to us so easily, a world where warmth, humor and sheer happiness reigned and where all activity was directed toward a single goal: how and in what way could he help everyone today?

Jan Maarten was permitted to live among us for far longer than we ever dared hope; and for this we shall always be grateful.